The Chronology Of Love

Khushi R Keerthy

BookLeaf Publishing
India | USA | UK

Made with ❤ on the BookLeaf Publishing Platform
www.bookleafpub.in
www.bookleafpub.com

Dedication

To the hopeless romantics and the one I haven't met yet.

Preface

Acknowledgements

Every page of this book is filled with emotions that most of us experience at least once in our lifetimes. This book would not have been possible without:

My parents, Satya Keerthy and Sindhuri Keerthy, for being the first people to show me what true love looks like.

My brother, Raghava, and my jiggiesss Tanisha, Shraddha, Kashvi and Varshini, who believed in me before I could.

Last but not least, Jyothsna, who has been nothing less than an editor to this book and a therapist to me.

1. Situationship

One foot in,
One foot out.
Always ready to leave
Just to run back to you.
I'm everywhere
And nowhere
When I'm with you.

2. Tale of not yet lovers

We think of each other in the dead of night,
But we steal glances in broad daylight.
Then, what are we?
Cowards who meet on dreamy nights,
Or brave to meet eyes in plain sight?

3. Favourite almost

You were my favourite almost
Like bitter coffee and almond toast,
Thinking that your sweetness
It could overpower my bitterness.
You were my favourite almost,
Like the light from the lamp post
That flickered on and off indecisively,
Pondering whether to illuminate or leave me blindly.
But alas, you remained the ghost of spring,
A beautiful butterfly with one wing,
Who loved the blue open sky
But never dared to fly.

4. What never was

We share the same fiery eyes
The one that rejects goodbyes,
But there was never a start
For us to take apart our heart.
I wish I had seized the moment.
I wish you had seized my hand.
But now we dance in the shadows
Forever lost in what never was.

5. Drought

I see you from far away,
And my eyes fill
With the rain of sadness.
Tell me how I drown
In this drought of love?

6. Conspiracy

My eyes conspire against me,
urging me to steal glances.
Your name haunts my lips,
teasing me to get drunk on it.
You've made me a thief, an addict,
And now all I do is drown in you.

7. Courage

The courage it took to look up
and find your gaze
was enough to fight
a 1000 battles within.
You picked the sword
And cut my heart in two.
The smaller belongs to me
And the bigger half to you.
The courage it took
For my lips to utter your name
Echoes deep into silence
And rings in my ear for centuries.
"God, I love you."
Your love came to me like a calamity
that even the lord's name
sounded like a profanity.

8. Restaurant

I always wonder why they play loud music in restaurants.
It's so that lovers can sit next to each other, whisper into each other's ears.

I always wonder why the lighting is so dim in restaurants.
It is because the only bright light is the one in their lover's eyes.

I always wonder why there is so much wine in restaurants.
It's to give lovers a little push to open their hearts to each other.

I always wonder why people end their nights with desserts in restaurants.
It's in hopes that this sweet night will lead to a new sweetheart.

9. Thief of sleep

With the onset of twilight,
Your crimes reach their height.
You become the thief of my sleep,
But your name becomes mine to keep.
Because now my soul will fight,
And all it'll ever want to write
Is the love it has for the thief of sleep
While it knows you'll leave my heart to weep.

In shadows deep, where your whispers creep,
I tread the line where secrets seep.
Your each sigh is a sonnet, each tear a line,
Yet in your gaze, I find a sign.
There's a fleeting touch, a stolen glance,
In my dreams, we dance—a wild romance.
Though dawn may steal you from my side,
In every heartbeat, you'll abide.

10. Candlelight

The wick burns higher,
With every night we're apart.
But the wait becomes sweeter,
And my heart burns brighter,
Just as I see your eyes
Before the candlelight fades away.

11. Garland

You left one flower behind
From the garland
You were wearing
In your hair
And with that,
You left me with
The smell of love
That will leave me
Intoxicated
For the rest of
Eternity.

12. Perfume of love

The pink petals of spring
Are scattered on the ground like my heart.
Will you keep it safe in your books,
Or sweep me off my feet?
The sweet scent of nectar
Engulfs my senses.
Is it the smell of flowers,
Or the perfume of love?

13. Seasons

I'll keep you warm in winter,
Fan you during summer,
Kiss you under the rain in monsoon,
Pick flowers for you in spring,
And I'll fall for you in fall.

14. Dots

Dot after dot
Memories collided
To form the line of life.

Dot after dot
Our souls came closer
to draw the portrait of our existence.

Line after line
We wrote the song
That we'll play in times of silence.

And Line after line,
We created paragraphs of love
that we will read to our future.

15. Tea Bags

I seep into you like a tea bag
In a steaming hot mug of water.
You change the way I see myself
Making me a dark, rich colour.
We mingle into each other
I, sharing my bitterness
You, diluting my taste,
Making me more salvageable
Making me more lovable, liveable.

16. Verses

With verses in our eyes
We spoke for decades.
I turned our conversation
Into poetry
You turned it against us.

17. Watercolour Eyes

You give me watercolour eyes.
You make me cry in shades of envy and lies.
We painted with red, crimson and hues of blue,
but I was breaking and you didn't even have a clue.
When the tears started running down my cheek,
I made the colours fade, and you made me weak.
I let you stain my body with love so fake,
and you just stood there and saw me break
with both the colours and my heart bleeding.

18. Strangers

We meet again.
But this time,
As strangers.
Our eyes intertwine,
And there's remorse in'em
For we let our minds
Take control of something
That belonged to our hearts

19. Polaroids

The memories we made
We captured them in polaroids.
But as the photos faded, so did you.

20. Servitude

Sleep lingers in my eyes
Your words ring in my ears
Your lips are engraved on my skin.
But I woke up feeling empty.
Cold.
How do I free myself
From the servitude of you?

21. Sketches

The flowers that I dried,
Between the pages of poetry
Still holds the fragrance of our young love.
In every petal lies the memory
Of our imagined fate.
Like the sketch of a flower,
I see your gentleness
Like the shading of the pencil
You surprise me every time
With your different shades.